Out c & Into the Sun

An Anthology of Poems and Stories from the Ladies of Lambda Beta Alpha Military Sorority, Incorporated

Dr. Tarama Giles · Dr. Deborah Ivey · Dr. Charlene Outterbridge-Meeks · Dr. Dana Thomas · Melissa Barnes · Queen Broussard · Donna Elliott · Tamara Singleton ·Tierney Stanley

Compiled by: Ladies Bonded in Arms

Edited by: Dr. Tarama Giles

DEDICATION

This collection of works is dedicated to all our sisters-in-arms from all branches of the United States military – Air Force, Army, Coast Guard, Marine Corps, Navy, Space Force, National Guard, and Reserves. We hear you; we see you; we have your six.

CONTENTS

ACKNOWLEDGMENTS

We give thanks to our supportive family and close friends who have been with us through our struggles. We appreciate your loyalty, dedication, and love. We would not make it to that light without you.

To all the Ladies of Lambda Beta Alpha Military Sorority, Inc, we are "united in service, bound by love".

1 DONNA ELLIOTT

I Am Somebody

My mother and father separated when I was young. As a result, we had to go and live in the rough projects of Washington, DC. Living and growing up in the projects let me know that I did not like that life, nor did I want to grow up in that environment.

I decided young that I was going to go to school and get a good education and take myself out of the projects. I was the first in my family to graduate from college. After I got my BSW degree, I set my mind on getting my MSW Degree. When I graduated from Howard University with my MSW Degree on that Saturday, I left for Basic Training on that Sunday. I had told myself that I would go into the Military. Going into the military was one of the best decisions I ever made. My MOS was 76Y.

Another goal I set was to get married and have kids. I am happy and proud to say that I have been married to a wonderful Navy Veteran for 33 years, and we have two grown kids. We have a son and a daughter.

While I was in college, I always wanted to pledge a sorority but didn't because of the hazing they did. I am proud to let everyone know that I just accomplished my goal of belonging to a sorority. I just crossed over as Lady Alexandra with the Lambda Beta Alpha Military Sorority, Incorporated. I am part of Dynasty XII (the 12th national line). I'm so glad to be part of a Military sorority that promotes sisterhood and is committed to helping our veteran community. I trusted the process and came *out of the shadows and into the* sun by joining this wonderful Sorority.

So, as you can see, I am somebody. I am fearfully and wonderfully made. I did not let my environment or upbringing keep me in bondage and a statistic.

Donna Elliott, a devoted wife, and mother of two, is a dynamic force, seamlessly blending her passion for social work with her love for culinary arts. Born in the heart of South Carolina, Donna was raised in the vibrant atmosphere of Washington, DC, where her journey of resilience and determination began.

Donna holds a bachelor's degree in social work from Morgan State University, laying the foundation for her commitment to community service and advocating for the well-being of families. Her academic pursuits continued at Howard University, where she earned a master's degree in social work, honing her skills to address the multifaceted challenges faced by individuals and families.

Currently employed by DC Child and Family Services, Donna is a dedicated professional with a heart for underprivileged children. Her service extends beyond the workplace, as she finds fulfillment in volunteering within her community and church. Donna's military service in the Army Reserve as a Unity Supply Specialist reflects her resilience and commitment to serving others.

Beyond her professional endeavors, Donna's diverse interests include cooking, baking, and reading. She finds solace in the simple joys of spending time with her family and appreciating the beauty of nature, often sitting on the beach to witness the breathtaking moments of sunrise and sunset.

Known for her strong-willed and outgoing nature, Donna is a friendly soul who believes in the uniqueness of every individual. She sees each person as a masterpiece created by God, embodying this philosophy in her interactions with others. Donna's love for sharing and feeding people has become a hallmark of her personality, creating a warm and welcoming atmosphere wherever she goes.

Looking toward the future, Donna envisions a long-term goal of establishing "Therapeutic Loving Care," a company where she can synergize her social work expertise and culinary skills to make a positive impact in the community. With her unwavering determination and passion for helping others, Donna Elliott is a shining example of the extraordinary possibilities that emerge when compassion meets purpose.

2 DR. DANA THOMAS

Unwavering Might

In the quiet of the night, I bear the weight of an alcoholic

husband, whether wrong or right. His uncertain state and the

bottle's grip are a relentless pull in our shared world of

emotions in turmoil.

His laughter, once music to my ears, was now dulled by

alcohol's relentless fears. But I still see the man, the one I adore,

beneath the mask, the struggles he can't ignore.

I've held his hand through the darkest times as he fought with

alcohol's relentless crimes. I see the man I love, not the bottle's

thread in every stumble, every tear he's shed.

The battles are tough, and the scars may linger and show, but the love within us continues to grow. Deep in his heart, a spirit persists, yearning for freedom from the alcohol's twists.

I won't give up, our love's not in vain. In his struggle, I know there's strength to regain. Though it's a rough journey, we'll find our way together and face the light of a brand-new day.

As long as there's love and hope in our sight, we'll confront this challenge with unwavering might. I'll stand by his side, through thick and thin, On the path to recovery; together, we'll win.

Dr. Dana Thomas, a retired veteran with an illustrious 30-year career in the United States Army, continues to serve with distinction as a Human Resource Specialist at the United States Army Reserve Command. Her journey, marked by dedication and service, extends beyond the military realm, showcasing her commitment to the community and the well-being of others.

A trailblazer in her own right, Dana is one of the founders of the Lambda Beta Alpha Military Sorority, a distinguished organization established on November 10, 2017. Fueled by the shared experiences of ten veteran women, the sorority became a vital platform for strengthening the bonds forged while in uniform, creating a sisterhood that transcends military service.

Dana's academic achievements include a master's degree in business administration with a concentration in Human Resources from Columbia Southern University. This educational background, coupled with her extensive military experience, positions her as a seasoned professional in her role as a Human Resource Specialist. She also has an honorary PhD in Business Entrepreneurship and a Business Coaching certificate from TIUA.

Beyond her professional accomplishments, Dana's personal mission speaks volumes about her character. In honor of her late grandmother, Helen Griffin, Dana aspires to open an adult daycare facility. Inspired by the care and compassion her mother provided to her grandmother until her passing, Dana envisions creating a space that embodies the same level of dedication and love.

Dana's story is a testament to resilience, leadership, and a profound commitment to making a positive impact on the lives of others. As an author, veteran, and advocate, Dana Thomas embodies the spirit of service and community, leaving an indelible mark on those who have had the privilege of crossing paths with this remarkable individual.

3 TIERNEY STANLEY

Into the Light

I'm surrounded by a room full of people, yet I am still alone.

Physically I'm present, but my mind is absent.

I laugh, almost on cue, to cloak my chaos.

To those around me, I'm engaged, but mentally I'm paralyzed

by my fears and my doubts.

A constant battle between darkness and light.

The darkness, an abyss of nothingness.

The Light is welcoming, with hands stretched wide.

Blindly, I walk through the nothingness, trying to catch a

glimmer of the warm and comforting Light.

The journey is long, and my body is tired.

I lay down in the stillness, cold and defeated.

In my slumber, a voice beckons me to take their hand

The voice tells me "Be not afraid."

My body becomes lighter as the hand pulls me toward the light.

The nothingness constantly tugs at me never letting free.

The struggle is ongoing, but I continue to fight to find my way

into the light.

Tierney M. Stanley, a proud native of Philadelphia,
Pennsylvania, was born on May 15 to her parents, Michael E.
Rogers (deceased) and Barbara Montague (formerly Rogers).
Her life is intricately woven with love, family, and a
commitment to service.

Currently residing with her mother, her college athlete son,
Jayden, pursuing a degree in Sports Management, and her
significant other, LaShawn, Tierney embodies the essence of a
dedicated family woman. Her journey as a veteran of the United
States Air Force has seamlessly transitioned into her role with
the Department of Veterans Affairs, where she has served in
Human Resources for the past eighteen years. In this capacity,
Tierney continues to contribute her skills and dedication to
support her fellow veterans.

Adding another layer to her rich tapestry, Tierney joined the
esteemed Lambda Beta Alpha Military Sorority, Incorporated in

the Winter of 2021. As part of the inaugural line for Alpha Chapter, Tierney, along with her six line sisters, made history for the sorority as the first group of ladies initiated into a chapter. Currently, she serves in the vital role of parliamentarian for Alpha Chapter and is an integral member of the Intake Committee, contributing to the growth and success of the sorority.

Beyond her professional and sorority commitments, Tierney finds solace and joy in spending quality time with her family, including childhood friends with whom she shares a bond that has endured for over 35+ years. Her adventurous spirit comes to life as she travels the world with LaShawn, exploring different countries and experiencing the beauty and diversity that the world has to offer.

Tierney M. Stanley is more than a veteran, a professional, and a sorority sister; she is a living testament to the power of connection, service, and the pursuit of meaningful experiences. Her story is one of resilience, love, and a commitment to making a positive impact on the lives of those around her.

4 DR. TARAMA GILES

A Silent Warrior's Struggle

She marches beside her brothers in uniform; she stands,

Yet the respect she's earned slips through an unseen hand.

Her deeds are bold, her sacrifices great,

But gender blinds the eyes, sealing an unjust fate.

On fields of war, she fought the same against a common foe,

But back on home terrain, a different battle would grow.

For through the uniform covers all in shades of green and tan,

Some still see not the soldier but a woman, less than a man.

She served with strength, with heart ablaze,

Yet societal norms cast a shadow on her days.

Her courage echoes, unheard, in a world that fails to see,

That valor knows no gender, it wears no boundary.

The parades may pass, the anthems play,

But her struggle lingers, hidden, day by day.

Equal in service, in sacrifice profound,

Yet inequality persists, an unspoken, deafening sound.

In the echoes of the barracks, in the silence of the night,

Her story whispers softly, seeking its own light.

A veteran, resilient, yet longing to be seen,

In a world that should recognize the strength within the sheen.

Let us peel away the bias, the stereotypes that bind,

For in unity and equality, true strength we find.

No longer a shadow but a warrior revealed,

Her story, like her spirit, cannot be concealed.

A female veteran, resilient and strong,

She deserves the same respect where she belongs.

In the tapestry of heroes, in the annals of the free,

May equality reign, for her, for you, for me.

Wash…Rinse…Repeat

It doesn't matter which branch of service you decide to enter, no one truly prepares you for what's to come. How can they? Everyone's experience is his/her own. Each MOS/AFSC comes with its own circumstances, and even with that, things differ. On any given day, situations and events may change. Don't get me wrong, there are certain similarities and shared experiences that make the military bonds even more special. It's just not a wash, rinse, and repeat world. Truth be told, that goes for pretty much anything in life. I'm just here to speak on my wash-dry cycle as a female veteran. Sometimes, a cycle can go perfectly, with clothes coming out smelling fresh and the warmth of the sun from being line-dried or the dryer making you want just to hold the item close to you as if it is exuding love.

Sometimes, a cycle can go absolutely, horribly wrong. Just when you think you're about to pull out some beautifully crisp, snow-white linen and clothes from the washer, you realize there are pink and blue stains where somehow you missed your fairly new red shirt and denim shorts that were balled up with the sheets when you put them in the laundry basket. Metaphorically, that's how many parts of my life have been. Some days were fresh, beautiful, and full of life, while others spent trying to recover from the stains.

Even though I come from an extensive line of military veterans on both sides of my family, I enlisted in the military pretty much on a dare. I was at my dad's house and my grandparents were visiting. Somehow, we got into a conversation about military life, which wasn't too out of the ordinary given that both my dad and granddad were retired Air Force vets. Ironically enough, no female on this side of the family had served. Now, I can't speak for distant cousins. I just know that none of my aunts, first or second cousins served. Well, the conversation turned to my bringing up a hypothetical - me joining the Air Force. I was "aware" of the life, having grown up with my mother and stepfather, who were both in the Air Force as well. I was used to the structure/discipline, some of the protocols, ranks, marching and facing movements, military bases, and a lot of the things military family members recognize and encounter. I was confident that I was ready. My granddad, Pop Pop as we called him, on the other hand, was none too shy or reluctant to offer up his thoughts on the matter. At first, he told me I couldn't go. As the patriarch of the family who was approximately 6'3" tall and over 300lbs, that would be intimidating to many. In all the respect I could muster because I did respect and love it, I disagreed with him. There I was 22 years old with a few years of college behind me telling my Pop Pop what I could and would do. I never took lightly to anyone telling me I couldn't do something.

Not being able to do something because of laws or the lack of something existing, like not having girls' volleyball or track teams in high school was one thing. (Sidenote: I didn't just take that either. I started petitions for both at school. They didn't manifest during my time, but I tried). Anyway, seeing I was unfazed and wasn't changing my mind, Pop Pop sat in the corner of the sectional closest to the patio door and began to tell me how I wouldn't make it. In my mind, all I could think of was - what kind of misogynistic thinking is this? Didn't he realize that it was 1996? Shouldn't he be happy that I was going to follow in their footsteps? Now that I think about it, maybe the latter is what crossed his mind, especially given the statements about my having inherited the attitude, mouth, and not being run over by anyone, no matter who, seniority or not. Apparently, both he and my dad had a run-in or two with some fellow servicemen during their time. At any rate, I wasn't trying to hear it. All I knew was that I was even more hellbent to go into the Air Force. I would enlist in the Radiology career field; go back to school since the military would pay for it; and prove Pop Pop all the way wrong. Remember, I opened by saying that no one can truly prepare you for what's to come.

To make a long backstory short, within a few days post the conversation, or better yet debate with my granddad, I went to the Air Force recruiter and told him I wanted to enlist for 4R0X1

- Diagnostic Imaging. I didn't have my degree yet, which ruled out going in as an officer; however, I had enough credits to go in as an E-3 (Airman First Class). I couldn't go in right away because the needs of the Air Force at that specific time didn't have a slot for the career field I wanted. It would mean going into the Delayed Entry Program. This was like pausing the washer to add in an item or two. In the grand scheme of things, the plan wasn't disrupted, just altered a little. I went to the Military Enlisted Processing Stations (MEPS), retook the ASVAB since it had been several years, and upon their review of my transcripts and seeing the several foreign languages I'd taken, was convinced the Defense Language Aptitude Battery (DLAB). Since I scored very well on the DLAB, I was informed that I "had to become a linguist". My not knowing better at the time led me to do just that. This is where the washing machine started to do that crazy rocking thing. This wasn't a part of my plan at all. Well, I had to make the best of it. There was no way I was going to let anything stop me from proving Pop Pop wrong. So, I signed the papers; raised my right hand to take the oath; and a couple of months later, there I was at Lackland Air Force Base getting yelled at with all the others under the overhang at o 'dark thirty by several men and women wearing blue Smokey the Bear hats and shoes that clicked when they walked. This was really happening.

The next couple of years went well. I mean, how can they not when you're at the Presidio of Monterey for the first part of tech school? Goodfellow Air Force Base, in all its remote feeling, wasn't so bad either. I met some amazing people from all over the country. Some of them with whom I still maintain some kind of communication. Pop Pop was surprised I made it through basic training, and unfortunately, he passed away too early in my military career to see my progression.

The events of September 11, 2001, are where the figuratively stained clothing and broken-down washers came into play. Much like the rest of the country, innumerable tears were shed, feelings of overwhelming helplessness crept in, and moments of anger, frustration, and confusion arose. What was happening, and what would this mean for my career? Had I known better, would I have fought to keep Radiology as my career of choice, or would I have stayed with being a linguist? I loved both the medical field and languages. What I hadn't mentioned yet was my language specialty. You see, in basic training, they had all the linguists meet up and make a list of the languages they wanted. I don't know why; it must be an inside joke because they soon gave us the list of languages that met the Air Force's needs. From there, we had to rank them. Well, let's just say I was originally given Korean, my third language of choice but fought to get Arabic, my first language of choice. I ended up getting Arabic, and I must admit that when September 11th hit, a part of me wished I'd kept Korean. It was fear setting in. While I knew and believed the oath I took, nothing truly prepared me for the transpiring events. You sign up knowing that something COULD happen. It's just a big wake-up call when it does.

Fast forward a couple of months, and I was on an airplane with a bunch of my fellow brothers and sisters-in-arms stationed at Langley Air Force Base and headed to Saudi Arabia. It wasn't my first time out of the country, just the first time under these circumstances. The stress of the unknown and hypervigilance surely takes a toll and, honestly, doesn't easily go away. Here I am, 22 years later, still affected by it. There were days I sat in my room crying, not because I was ready to go home but because of the state of the world. Being a feeling empath doesn't help at all. I just knew that I had to do my part to help protect my home country from enemies both foreign and domestic. In my free time, I hung out with some of the people I befriended as well as joined the gospel choir. Those were two of the things I truly cherished and needed to help with my sanity.

Over the years since the deployment, the breakout of the war in Iraq, and the things I've seen, it was like going out of the frying pan into the oven. To top it off, I was a single mother and the threat of a possible second deployment hovered like the Grim Reaper. While I loved the Air Force, I was at a crossroads. I had to make the decision of staying in and risk deploying again, this time leaving my child behind or getting out and starting my new life as a civilian. It wasn't an easy decision because I'm never one just to quit. This war was something I'd never seen before. When I didn't make TSgt, I used that as a sign that it was time to go. I would be looking at 11 years, which, given the time and world events, was a considerable amount of time. So, in January 2008, I was done.

The thing is, when you've seen unspeakable things, you're never "done". On top of the hypervigilance, you become afraid to sleep, and sleep deprivation leads to other issues. For years, I dealt with stress, anxiety, depression, and nightmares and felt I had nowhere to turn. Back then, there was a stigma associated with seeking help for mental health issues. We were always told that we would lose our security clearance if we went to see a psychologist or psychiatrist. It wasn't until 2016 when this Godsend informed me that wouldn't be the case. On top of dealing with PTSD and everything else, I was dealing with a very short-lived first marriage to a man who decided he was going to up and leave one day and never come back. Not to mention, we were homeless and living in a friend's basement because my home sold faster than expected, and we couldn't move into the new home that was nearly finished. I had all kinds of suicidal thoughts. I was seconds from downing a bottle of pills when I looked over at my sleeping kids and broke down crying. I sent my therapist a message letting her know that I needed to see her the very next day. Unbeknownst to my kids, they saved my life that night. The next day, I had to start tackling those stains bit by bit.

Due to the nature of some of the stains, I would never get past the surface; however, doing that did help. Sure, it would be easy just to throw out everything and buy new. That is just a quick fix, though, because you haven't addressed the problem. You're smart enough to know that these stains were scars. Scars, which are continuing to heal.

Just as I mentioned in the beginning, no one can truly prepare you for what's to come when you join the military. Again, this was just a part of my journey. It wasn't all bad. I would be lying if I said so. I'm merely touching upon some of the darkness I went through. There are still triggers; however, I am in a better place to recognize what they are and try my best not to put myself in situations where I would regress. I guess you can say that I have gotten better at sorting my laundry. I find my sunshine by writing and crafting. I have my Emotional Support Animal, who is of tremendous help. As I write, she is lying right next to me, and we are both just as content as can be. Even with hanging out this proverbial laundry, I can smell the crisp, fresh linen and see the bright colors. We'll see what tomorrow holds. That's the key, taking each day as it comes. This is where the wash, rinse, repeat comes into play because I've found a rhythm. I hope you find yours.

Dr. Tarama Giles is the visionary behind Lambda Beta Alpha Military Sorority, Incorporated. With a rich background that weaves together military service, corporate experience, and a passion for community building, Tarama has become a prominent advocate and leader in various spheres.

Having served in the Air Force for 11 years, Tarama then transitioned into the private sector, accumulating over 15 years of invaluable experience. Her educational journey reflects her diverse interests, with a Bachelor of Science degree in Arabic, a Master of Arts degree in Criminal Justice, and the recent addition of an honorary Ph.D. in Business Entrepreneurship and Business Coaching Certificate.

As a bestselling author, Tarama, under the pseudonym Naomi J. Colington, has recently released two children's books, "Just For Me" and "Watch It Grow: A Look into a Sibling Relationship." She has also made significant contributions to anthologies such as "Beyond Boundaries: Inspiring Leaders in Business and Community" and "The Forgotten Queens: You Are Not Forgotten; You Are Loved."

In addition to her literary pursuits, Tarama is deeply committed to community service and advocacy. A strong voice for mental health services and improved health avenues for veterans, she champions causes that resonate with her fellow sisters-in-arms. Beyond Lambda Beta Alpha., Tarama has been a member of Alpha Kappa Alpha Sorority, Incorporated for 16 years.

Tarama Giles is a loving mother to two beautiful children and the proud owner of an American Pitbull. She is the CEO of Rayne Books LLC and working on the launch of Phoenix Leadership and Legacy Consulting. Her journey is a testament to the power of resilience, continuous learning, and a passion for making a positive impact in the lives of others.

.

5 QUEEN BROUSSARD

When the Light Goes Out.

When the light goes out, I won't be tired. Because this life that I have lived has caused me to shake tired off. Unable to complain, had to press through this pain, no matter what.

When the light goes out, I won't sit down. Too many times I had to hide my frown yet stand my ground when I wanted to sit and run, when I wanted to lay around.

When the light goes out, I won't say a word. Too many times when I wanted to speak up, I was muzzled to ensure I wasn't heard.

When the light goes out, I won't accuse. I had the same number of opportunities to make something of myself. Win or lose.

When the light goes out, I won't stress. I thank God for every adversity that was allowed in my life. I wouldn't ask him for more, and I wouldn't ask Him for less.

When the light goes out, I will be grateful, never hateful, because I have seen some things that would make the devil scream. Things that would make one question their value, but I had to remind myself that day after day, no matter what the battle, no matter what the war. I have the tools to prevail.

When the light goes out, the world will attempt to divide, try to make me hide my intellect and my pride. Everything that I have been built to build will hold up long after I am gone.

When the light goes out, there will be a legacy that was built on my tenacity and my ability to turn the other cheek. I remember when they called me a freak. Of this nature or unnatural because I could see past one's intent and deep into the root of the matter. But that made me sadder than I could ever explain. How could I be ungrateful for the gift?

When the light goes out, I will have pressed for the mark and left a mark behind that says I was kind in spite of the warfare. The world doesn't care, but I do. Looking in the

mirror, knowing that there is more inside you. Not bowing to
the blows of life that come upon you.

When the lights go out. I will step out of the shadows with
power in my fight. I will be the salt and the light. Called to be
difference where evil is all the same. He will say a good job; you
did it in My name. Heaven bound. When the lights go out.

M.U.D. T.H.U.G

I don't look like the hell, I have been through. No really, I don't. I am layers of a woman who has been through some things. And at the end of the day, I am still going through. When people look at me from the outside. They all have their interpretations of who I am, my background, and all the possible things that could have made me what I am today. But at the end of the day. I am proud to say. I am a **MUD– THUG**.

Who wants to openly admit that they were made under the worst conditions? Made in the mud? I know that even though I have served my country, retired, and am a broken-up disabled veteran, many would disagree because I never touched foreign soil, at least not on active duty, only as a Military Brat. That's where the confusion is. You don't have to go far to find your enemy. Because your enemy most times will come and find you. The soil that I have walked on for the majority of my days has been the place where I have found the greatest wars in my life. With the people that I have held the dearest and the closest, or people who have never interacted with me but just "something about me." Or worse, there have been the greatest frenemies of my life. For some reason, it has been their goal to find the things that have been the most important to me, to infiltrate my life, my heart, and my babies, and those are the things that they attack first, to strip away from me.

I have always been different, and it has never been intentional. I am easygoing and helpful. You can pretty much talk to me about any and everything. You can put me in any environment, and I will thrive. I love everyone and everything until they come for me, or the things that I love, or they have proven loyal to my demise. It wasn't until I stared down an empty glass of poison that I realized that someone I loved more than my very life itself was willing to end it before they let someone else have me.

You don't realize how much you want to live until you stare death in the face when you didn't call for him. Thankfully, the first law of nature is self-preservation. We are equipped with minds, bodies, souls, wills, and emotions that assist us in survival. A lot of people don't know it, but perception is really our reality. Perception comes from the Latin word Perceptio or Percipere. They mean to seize or understand. Forgive me, but it's the teacher in me. What is crazy, no pun intended is that the psychology perspective is that it is the "neurophysiological process, including memory, by which an organism becomes aware of and interprets external stimuli." In other words, your internal perception of anything becomes part of your neurological interpretation, which affects your response to what is happening to you externally. What you perceive a thing to be, is what it is.

Your success, your failure, your health, your sickness. Your direction in life, your faith, your vision and dreams, your rise, your downfall. How you physically and emotionally handle a situation is what it is. If you perceive your life ending. It will end. If you fight and believe, your neurological system fights and believes with you, and it tells the rest of your body to obey and follow suit. Obviously, it's not that easy, or we would all be healthy, strong, and bulletproof. We have been encouraged a million times and still need to be encouraged.

It's in your DNA and your spirit, man, to fight and survive. The hardest battle to fight is an unseen enemy or to be a naïve person who doesn't know that an enemy exists. Until one day, I picked up the bible and read this scripture. Ephesians 6:11-18 "Put on the whole armor of God..." When I began to fully understand what this scripture was saying. It changed and began to transform my life. I became and will always be a MUD THUG.

MADE UNDER DISTRESS, TOTALLY HUMBLE UNDER GOD

I am *MUD – I was made under distress.* There were lots of situations where I was supposed to be crushed, cracked, or even broken and destroyed. When situations arose with the fight or flight and most people fled, I came out swinging. I had no fear in my heart to fight a man or a woman. If you came with it, my crew and I would fight you, and if we lost, you would have to fight us every time you saw us. NO matter the environment, even if I was wrong. I would immediately deal with my adversary because I let him handle me over half my life. I had to learn to be a better version of myself, whether in public or in private. Integrity has always been important to me. I am the same person in front of people as I am when I am by myself in private. One thing I learned quickly in this life is that I desire to live; I desire to survive. I desire to see the greatness in me in the promises of God.

I am a *THUG, Totally Humble, Under God.* I am certain that although I don't share all my stories, I wasn't always nice and sweet. I wasn't always the one you would want on your team. But I was not one you wanted as an opponent either. People were allowed to live their lives and walk their paths as long as they didn't cross mine the wrong way. I could verbally make the proudest man run with his tail between his legs. I was the emasculation QUEEN. I had NO love for mankind after the betrayal, deceit, and anger I felt. They said hell hath no fury like a woman scorned, but what they don't tell you is that fury fire is burning inside and out, and if you don't unleash it or put it out. It will kill you.

SURVIVAL OF THE FITTEST

I am a survivor - An airman falling off the top and being left for dead under a Tank during a training exercise; because I was in the Air Force and my army cohorts excluded me from the training to get in and out of a tank, driving off while getting in, and they thought it was funny! I am a survivor of being raped and attacked by a soldier during my tech school training because my battle buddy decided to leave me behind. I am a survivor of being abandoned with two children and being homeless for three months. I am a survivor of being in a relationship prison for over seven years, with at least two attempts on my life. I am a survivor of being robbed twice, once by gunpoint, the other by knife. I am a survivor of 12 years of being looked over, passed over, and shuffled around to avoid being promoted or celebrated because "I was a go-getter but should not be doing better than the fellas, give them a chance to shine." I am a survivor of 3 car accidents, one of which was head-on. I am a survivor of four childbirths, three of whom survived when doctors said I could never have children. Daily, I survive despite the physical, emotional, spiritual, and financial wounds I have faced in my life. Without God, His word and an ear to hear, I would be DEAD and gone.

I have never told my whole story to this date. Only fragments because it's a lot, and it's heartbreaking. I don't want anyone to feel sorry for me, I don't feel sorry for myself. I realized whatever I endure is either to be a blessing or to prepare me for the blessing that is coming my way. A MUD THUG is one that is hidden from its environment. Covered in distress, covered in the shadows, hanging in the back, I don't stand up and toot my own horn; I stand up when I am called to function, and then I go sit back down. Everything I do is for a purpose because I understand that God has called me to it. My past, or my mud, covers me until I rise up out of the shadows and remind the devil why I was the wrong one to ever stir up. When I wasn't saved, the things I used to do, the hell I raised, the people who still cross the street when they see me today. All in the past.

One thing is for certain. Who I do it for is GOD and GOD alone. So, if you see me sitting quietly in the back. Allow me to simmer in my MUD. When the Shadows can no longer hold me, I'm coming out.

Queen Broussard, born on May 8th to Coy and Melody Burleson, is a multifaceted individual whose life is a tapestry of family, entrepreneurship, service, and a relentless pursuit of knowledge. As a loving mother of three, a proud grandmother, and a cherished son-in-law to her credit, Queen's life is enriched by the bonds she shares with her close-knit family.

Educationally equipped with a bachelor's degree in health sciences, Queen brings her expertise to the professional realm as a Human Resource Specialist for the Department of Treasury. Her career is a testament to her commitment to excellence and service in various capacities.

Beyond her role in the government sector, Queen is a serial entrepreneur, demonstrating her versatility and business acumen. She is the owner of TRUSTORI LLC CONSULTING, a venture that handles end-state planning, notary, and transcription. Additionally, she is the proud owner of The BEEZ-needs, a thrift "Swap Meet," and the co-owner of QueZai (pronounced QUEEZY) – Lemonade/Tea, a business with a mission to "Change the world one cup at a time."

Bold and charismatic, Queen identifies as an ambivert, seamlessly balancing her vocal presence with a deep well of love and care for her family and close friends. Her passion for teaching and learning extends to the practical and realistic exploration of the Bible, where she empowers others to see beyond their perceptions and tap into the wisdom of life.

Queen's list of accomplishments is impressive and varied, including a fulfilling journey of motherhood, grandmotherhood, and service in the Retired Air Force. She serves as the Chaplain of WVCT "Women Veterans of Central Texas" and holds the esteemed role of Scribe Minister. Her voice reaches far and wide as a Radio Personality for KRGN on "The Son's Cup" and "Midday - Reign with the Queen." Currently, she is the creator of the SOTM/SOTMWAR Blog, a platform where she shares her insights and wisdom with the world.

In Queen Broussard, one finds a dynamic individual whose life reflects a commitment to family, entrepreneurship, and the empowerment of others. Her journey is an inspiration, illustrating the transformative power of resilience, boldness, and a genuine love for life.

6 DR. DEBORAH IVEY

I Was Me

I left home at 17 to see the world and make a better life for
myself.

I had to grow up fast.

While everyone was celebrating a milestone birthday. I was
on KP duty washing big pots bigger than me.

I didn't have access to weapons, but in the military, I did.

I didn't have any idea of what gas was. Being in basic
training, I soon found out what it was.

Before you could come out, you had to do facing movements
and say your name, all while being a snotty mess.

Did I say I had to grow up fast? I had to be responsible and
take accountability because I belonged to Uncle Sam now.

I couldn't cry and say I wanted to go home because I raised
my right hand for my country. There was no turning back.

I had a point to prove. I was me, and I was strong.

Even though I was weak in my upper body, I stayed in the fight, determined not to give up. I was determined to see it through because I was me.

I learned so much away from home. I learned that I could do what I could do because I was me.

I had my first drink of beer in the military as we passed the range. I know that wasn't for me because of who I am.

I came home stronger and wiser because I was me.

The military made me grow up to be who I am today. It is who I am because I am me.

I joined the military to have a better life for myself because I grew up living in the projects of Washington, DC. My mom was a single parent with four children. Being in the military gave me an opportunity to grow into the person I am today. I was 17 when I joined the US Army and turned 18 while in Basic Training. It was a rainy day, and we were on the range. Luckily, I was on KP duty that day, so I stayed dry that day.

I have truly enjoyed my time in the military. There were so many good times and some not-so-good times. I have made some great connections in the military with lifelong friendships. The bad times I experienced in the military were being sexually harassed. He was the NBC Sgt who was married but wouldn't take no for an answer. I started feeling so uncomfortable going to the NBC room to conduct any kind of business. I tried to make sure I was never alone with him. I spoke to the Supply Sgt about it because we fell under him. His response was men are going to be men, and he basically didn't do anything. I got transferred to the Motor Pool and talked to the Motor Pool Sgt about it. I can honestly say he spoke to the NBC Sergeant about it, and he stopped the harassment. It also got me blacklisted, and people stopped talking to me. I was the victim, so why did I get treated that way? I didn't do anything wrong. That's why people don't come forward and suffer in silence. People feel like they have no way out of the situation, and they find it easier to kill themselves. Problem solved, right?

I got a chance to travel and go to school while in the military. No one could ever take my military experience from me because I earned it. You take the good with the bad. The gas chamber, the road marches with the rucksacks on your back. Sleeping in tents and sleeping in vehicles makes you appreciate what you have. The military has changed from when I first went in. I didn't like the way things were going, so I was glad when I was offered an early retirement because of medical issues. I retired in October of 2010 and have not looked back. I missed the people in my unit because we were like family. I was stationed at Ft Meade at a Maintenance Company. I was an Automated Logistics Specialist, and I didn't really do that job because I was always pulled to do administrative work in HQs. I worked in retention in my unit, as well as one of the NCOs conducting random urinalysis.

I would encourage any young person who doesn't have a plan after they graduate high school to join the military. You will gain some structure and leadership skills and be confident. You will also have a chance to go to school without racking up a lot of student loan debt. There is the chance to travel on the military's dime. There are pros and cons to everything. You make it work for you.

Dr. Deborah Ivey is a dynamic author and certified coach dedicated to inspiring and empowering women on their journey to reaching their fullest potential. Her impactful writing and coaching work are a testament to her commitment to building confidence and motivating others to show up boldly in their lives.

As the author of "Overcoming the Odds" and "My New Bold Journal: A Woman's Path to Showing Up Boldly for Christ," Deborah's literary contributions extend beyond these empowering works. She has coauthored six books and is currently involved in two other book projects: "121 Days of Prayer: 365 Affirmations from Around the World," "Tapping into Your Inner Beauty," "Daily Devotional II," "Your Wings Were Ready But My Heart was Not," "I Told the Storm", and "Finding Joy in your Journey Devotional."

Deborah's dedication to her craft is underscored by her extensive certifications. She is a Women's Empowerment Coach, Certified Leadership Coach, Certified Professional Speaker, and

Certified International Entrepreneur Coach through the Professional Woman's Network. Additionally, she holds certifications as a Life Coach, Pre-Marital and Marriage Coach (Hiscoach), and Christian Life Coach.

In 2023, Deborah's achievements were further recognized with an Honorary Doctorate Degree from TIUA and a Business Coaching Certificate. Her commitment to service and excellence has earned her the prestigious Presidential Lifetime Achievement Award.

Beyond her professional pursuits, Deborah is known for her passionate advocacy for others. She actively encourages women to express their feelings through journaling and generously gives away journals without expecting anything in return. Her dedication to community service is evident in her monthly involvement in food giveaways and her contributions to hygiene kits for homeless shelters. Notably, during the pandemic, Deborah donated funds to schools to support children whose families were unable to afford lunch.

Dr. Ivey's life and work embody a profound commitment to uplifting and supporting others. Through her writing, coaching, and acts of kindness, she leaves an indelible mark on the lives of those fortunate enough to encounter her wisdom and compassion.

7 MELISSA BARNES

This Race

For the time you were denied any personal leave,

Cuz a miscarried child need not be bereaved.

For the whistles and catcalls and other such noise.

'Ignore it,' they said, because 'boys will be boys.'

For promotions withheld and positions unfilled

'You can't do this job, certainly not with that build.'

When your home is a battlefield, you'd rather be deployed

Than to deal with that drunk when they're feeling 'annoyed.'

When the VA can't help; you're just too complicated

Because your scars are invisible, can't be medicated.

When "I AM the sponsor" tastes like ash in your mouth;

And you feel like you'll scream if they ask again 'bout your
spouse.

When you reported the harassment, asked for help up the
chain…
But what you got instead was a coffin laid to rest in the rain.

You knew your decisions could mean life or death,
But who knew the word 'help' would mean your last breath?

I see you, my sister. I mourn you, my friend.
I promise, I promise, this won't be the end.

See this vetHERan will fight till there's nothing left to do,
But to put down in law better protections for you.

I'll be standing the watch, ever vigilant and true.
You were owed so much more; yes, the system failed you.

I won't forget your name; I'll always remember your face
Until justice is served, I'll keep running this race.

I was in the middle of an online prenatal yoga instructor certification course when I had a complete breakdown.

The class's primary goal was to teach yoga instructors how to guide expectant mothers into safe and restorative yoga poses throughout their pregnancy. Part of the practice was mindful meditation, focusing loving thoughts and feelings on the child growing inside a future mom's womb.

At the conclusion of this particular practice, a portion of the guided meditation directed mom to place her hands on her abdomen and whisper gently - sending love, hope, and any dreams she had down into her womb to her tiny, innocent baby.

Suddenly, the pain and tightness I felt in my chest were so strong – I was completely overwhelmed. There I was, outwardly sobbing there, on camera, in front of my seven classmates and the master instructor. Tears running down my face, I finally had to acknowledge a belief that had been at the core of my being my entire life. I had been unwanted.

In those two minutes of meditation, I realized that deep in my heart and mind, in a place I'd kept hidden – even from myself, I truly believed that I needed to earn love. Because my teen mom

46

had to sacrifice so much just to get me to adulthood, I knew I had to do something *really* important for her sacrifice to have meant something. That she'd somehow hurt less and not lament her lost future because I would prove I had been worth it. Subconsciously, I had carried this invisible responsibility to every task, relationship, and goal. Life's purpose, needs, wants, and desires. All of it. All my life.

If you asked her, my mother would tell you that I was her constant. The thing that was always there, even when the rest of the world crashed down around her, she had me. When her father disowned her, her teen husband left her to "go find work" in the city (and never returned or sent the money he promised), and she struggled to find food for us - she always said I wasn't a mistake. That me being born just made her life *different*. But that word – different - carried so much weight in my subconscious. I could not imagine how, at just 18 years old, she did it. I knew that no matter how much she loved me, she had to resent what I'd done to her life.

See, even as a little kid, I knew that *different* didn't mean *worse*, but it also didn't mean *better*. I remember asking her once what she wanted to be before she had me. Architect, she said. I remember trying to imagine my mom designing buildings and skyscrapers. Instead, I saw her struggle at a grocery store in the produce section and, later, as a baker. Breaking her body, working long hours, frustrated and tired. My heart broke for her because I knew she *had* to have wanted more.

So, when she remarried a man I call dad, I knew that to be loved, I had to perform. Neither of my parents told me this – but I knew. If I could be perfect, then I couldn't be unlovable. Decades of straight A's, military service, multiple degrees, rapid promotions at work, all of it came crashing down. At age 44, after surviving war, my own divorce, and a million other forgotten hurts – here I was, crying about imaginary baby me and my mom feeling her tummy and wishing she had made different choices.

So, I cried. A lot. I tried to imagine how my life's choices might have been different if I hadn't pressured myself so much to please everyone – to be perfect in order to be loved. I know that we cannot change the past; all we have is the present, this very moment – and this one, and the next. Dwelling on those choices won't bring about a new today or a better tomorrow. The only way to do that is to remember that I am loved unconditionally by a higher power. That I was made, perfectly – there are no mistakes. There are no unwanted babies. Just imperfect people doing their best to love like this cosmic force does – unconditionally.

Melissa L. Barnes, originally from Medford, Oregon, has embraced the vibrant landscape of Indianapolis, Indiana, where she resides as a devoted wife, bonus mom to three incredible adult children and a retiree from the United States Air Force. Her journey is a captivating blend of service, resilience, and a commitment to holistic wellness.

A true advocate for the interconnectedness of body and mind, Melissa is not only an animal lover and a yoga instructor but also a passionate wellness and fitness advocate. She firmly believes that a healthy body nurtures a healthy mind, and a healthy mind is the foundation for building a better world.

Professionally, Melissa has dedicated her efforts to supporting veterans and government organizations in the realm of mental health awareness and advocacy. Her impact extends beyond her military service, as she has served as a Court Appointed Special Advocate (CASA) for foster children in the state of Georgia. This role, she describes, was both humbling and rewarding, leaving an indelible mark on her commitment to service.

Melissa's spiritual journey is marked by a triumphant overcoming of depression and anxiety. Prioritizing her health and family, she attests, was the most crucial decision she ever made. The transformational shift in her mindset, where she recognized her worthiness of love, rest, and joy, altered the trajectory of her life. Now, helping others find peace, balance, and clarity has become her life's work.

A notable accomplishment in Melissa's journey is the co-founding of Lambda Beta Alpha Military Sorority, Inc. Alongside nine other remarkable women, she has played a pivotal role in shaping the direction of the organization. Melissa expresses daily awe at its progress and eagerly anticipates the future of this exceptional sisterhood.

Melissa L. Barnes is not just an author but a living testament to the power of resilience, holistic well-being, and the transformative impact of a life dedicated to service and self-discovery. Her story is an inspiration to those seeking peace, balance, and purpose in their own journeys.

8 DR. CHARLENE OUTTERBRIDGE-MEEKS

S.H.E

It was like we always shadowed Them
Or should I say "Him"

The male figure that only some deemed worthy enough to serve
And yes got the medals that "She" so rightfully Deserved

Yet we raised our hand, took the same oath, got wounded,
harassed, fought in wars, and some women left children to take
far away from home tours

Fought for years and still fighting to come out of the shadow
and into the Sun. You see "She" I'll make sure you see "Her"
because the truth is this war has just begun

Yes, we are She, Her, Mrs., Ms., Miss
but this time, you won't get a chance to
kiss us goodbye or
dismiss us ... goodbye

Because we are here to stay.
We are Women with a Force, armed to serve every day

Dr. Charlene N. Outterbridge stands as a beacon of inspiration, a proud owner, a dedicated philanthropist, and a multifaceted professional whose journey weaves through various realms of service and entrepreneurship. As the owner of People's Choice Services LLC, an Insurance Agency, and the founder of "We Are the Children," an organization addressing the needs of children who lost a parent due to violence, Dr. Outterbridge's commitment to positive change and community welfare is palpable.

Her book, "You Will Get Through This...It Was All Necessary," serves as a testament to her journey and her desire to uplift others. Dr. Outterbridge's career path has been diverse, ranging from entrepreneurship and nursing to notary public, insurance agent, realtor, missionary, and youth pastor. Her love for helping people, inspiring greatness, and fostering positive change has driven her through these varied roles.

A distinguished graduate of Audenried High School, where she graduated as valedictorian, Dr. Outterbridge continued her academic journey at Temple University as a White-Williams Scholar. Her pursuit of knowledge extended to Calvary's Cross

Institute, where she earned a Ph.D.H of Humanity. She also has an honorary Ph.D. in Business Entrepreneurship and a Business Coaching certificate from TIUA. Additionally, she served in the United States Air Force, adding a military dimension to her rich and varied career.

As a missionary, Dr. Outterbridge has traveled to India, Africa, Dubai, and Mexico, embodying her commitment to global service. Professionally, she is affiliated with esteemed organizations such as The National Association of Professional Women, the National Association of Realtors, the Greater Philadelphia Association of Realtors, White-Williams Scholars, and CBNC (Treasurer). She is actively involved in charitable organizations, including Order of the Eastern Star – DGC, Heroines of Jericho, DOI, and proudly serves as the President of Alpha Chapter in Lambda Beta Alpha Military Sorority Inc.

Recipient of numerous awards for excellent service and dedication, Dr. Outterbridge is not only a successful professional but also a devoted wife to Kenyon Meeks and a loving mother to Shaleekqua Williams, Bralen, and Kyshaan Meeks. A Believer in Christ, she serves as the Youth Director at COTLG SM-K.

Dr. Charlene N. Outterbridge's life scripture, Philippians 4:13, encapsulates her unwavering spirit: "I can do all things through Christ which strengthens me." Her life's journey is an inspiration, a testament to resilience, faith, and the transformative power of service to others.

9 TAMARA SINGLETON

SARAH

As a little girl, she gave us change for the candy store

And for the chilly-bear lady

Enough for all her grandchildren, whom she treated the same

My love for her will always remain
A working woman with a great big heart
With gold, silver, and pearls overflowing

Her jewelry boxes
A closet filled with suits and hats
And shoes of all colors to match
Crawling out of bed to make it to church
No matter how much she may have hurt
We all loved Sarah with all our hearts

And when she became sick, I prayed that she wouldn't depart

Always a giver, this I know

As i received my last gift from her on June 6, 1994
The f blessing of not watching her close her eyes

For the final time

For she passed away before my plane arrived
You see, it was a hectic day of sorts
This day is the day of her birth

But it was also the day we gave her back to the earth

Rebirth

CHANCES

When your lonely heart is breaking

And your tears have been exhausted

But the pain still lingers there

Take it to the mender, commit it all to him

For Underneath, the burden

Your spirit cries aloud

Jesus' ear is in tune

He will hear your wails above the crowd.

Give it to him; Give him your heart

When he beckons you to come to him

Do not delay, today is the day

He has never left you

Even when you went astray

Give it to him

Do not delay, today is the day!

Tamara Singleton is a beacon of dedication and service, having proudly served and retired from the United States Army with almost 27 years of honorable commitment. Her journey, marked by resilience and passion, extends beyond her military service, defining her as a devoted mother, an advocate, and a passionate volunteer.

As a dedicated mom to her 19-year-old son, Devin, Tamara's commitment to family is at the core of her identity. She earned her Bachelor of Science degree in Human Resource Management from the University of Maryland, Global Campus, showcasing her commitment to personal and professional growth.

Tamara is not only a veteran but also an advocate for the rights of individuals with Down Syndrome and special needs. Her advocacy work is a testament to her compassionate spirit and commitment to creating a more inclusive and supportive society.

Currently serving as the secretary in Lambda Beta Alpha's Delta Chapter, Tamara actively contributes to the sorority's mission and values. Her involvement in various community organizations reflects her dedication to making a positive impact. Tamara volunteers with The York Area Down Syndrome Association, Special Olympics of York County, Friends of Lebanon Cemetery, Soldiers' Angel, Kingdom Hope Ministry, and more.

A proud member of American Legions #261 and #791 and the Disabled American Veterans, Tamara exemplifies the spirit of service and camaraderie. Her contributions extend beyond the military and veterans' organizations, as she actively engages in community service and outreach.

Tamara's commitment to uplifting others is further demonstrated in her role as a contributing author of a book of affirmations. Through her words and actions, she seeks to inspire and encourage those around her.

In Tamara Singleton, one finds not just a veteran, but a compassionate advocate, devoted mother, and community leader. Her life's journey is a testament to the transformative power of service and the positive impact one individual can make in the lives of others.

U.S. Air Force

Melissa Barnes
Queen Broussard
Dr. Tarama Giles
Dr. Charlene Outterbridge-Meeks
Tierney Stanley

U.S. Army

Dr. Deborah Ivey
Dr. Dana Thomas
Tamara Singleton

U.S. Army Reserve

Donna Elliott

"God is within her; she will not fall."

Psalm 46:5

LAMBDA BETA ALPHA
MILITARY SORORITY, INCORPORATED

ABOUT LAMBDA BETA ALPHA

The authors are all members of Lambda Beta Alpha Military Sorority, Incorporated, which is a 501(c)(3) organization founded on November 10, 2017, by ten veterans who were seeking a way to strengthen their bond as Sisters-in-Arms.

The mission of Lambda Beta Alpha is to foster sisterhood among a consummate group of exclusively chosen women from all branches of the United States Armed Forces; provide philanthropic and charitable services; study and promote awareness of women veteran issues; and share resources with young ladies entering the military as well as providing outreach and support to our sisters-in-arms who are separating or retiring from the military.

The proceeds from this book go towards Lambda Beta Alpha's Vet*H.E.R.*an national program. As such, your purchase is tax-deductible.

Made in the USA
Coppell, TX
27 December 2023

26945438R00046